3 in 1

(A Picture of God)

WRITTEN BY JOANNE MARXHAUSEN
ART BY BENJAMIN MARXHAUSEN

Publishing House
St. Louis London

Concordia Publishing House, St. Louis, Missouri
Concordia Publishing House Ltd., London E. C. 1
Copyright © 1973 Concordia Publishing House
International Standard Book No. 0-570-03419-1

HERE IS 1 APPLE.

THERE IS ONLY **1** TRUE GOD.

3

THE APPLE HAS THREE PARTS:

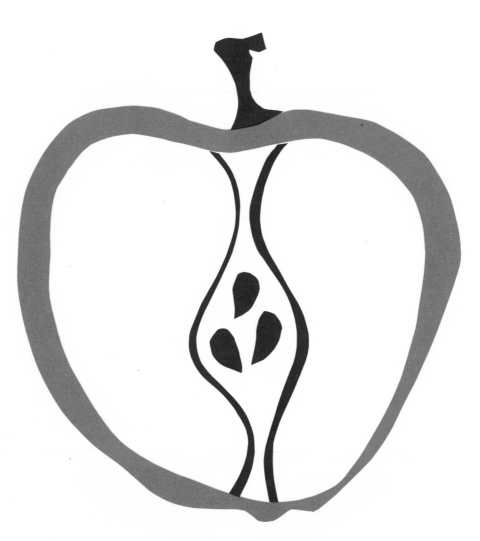

THE PEEL

THE FLESH

THE CORE.

THE 1 TRUE GOD HAS THREE PERSONS:

GOD THE FATHER

GOD THE SON

GOD THE HOLY SPIRIT.

ALL THREE PARTS OF THE APPLE ARE   APPLE.

THE PEEL IS   APPLE.

IT IS NOT ORANGE.
IT IS NOT BANANA.

THE FLESH IS   APPLE.

IT IS NOT PEAR.
IT IS NOT PLUM.

THE CORE IS   APPLE.

IT IS NOT GRAPEFRUIT.
IT IS NOT WATERMELON.

6

BUT THESE THREE:

PEEL

FLESH

CORE

ARE NOT THREE APPLES

BUT JUST APPLE.

ALL THREE PERSONS OF THE 1 TRUE GOD ARE GOD.

GOD

THE FATHER IS

GOD.

GOD

THE SON IS

GOD.

GOD

THE HOLY SPIRIT IS

GOD.

BUT THESE THREE:

FATHER   SON   HOLY SPIRIT

ARE NOT THREE GODS

BUT JUST 1 GOD.

THE THREE PARTS OF THE APPLE
HAVE DIFFERENT PURPOSES.

THE PEEL PROTECTS.

IT KEEPS THE APPLE HEALTHY.

THE FLESH OF THE APPLE

IS GOOD TO EAT.

LOTS OF GOOD THINGS
TO EAT ARE MADE FROM THE
FLESH OF THE APPLE.

APPLE PIE

APPLE CRISP

APPLE SAUCE

APPLE CIDER

APPLE
DUMPLINGS

APPLE JELLY

APPLESAUCE
CAKE

APPLE
FRITTERS

THE CORE OF THE APPLE

CONTAINS SEEDS FROM WHICH

APPLE TREES GROW.

WHEN JUST 1 APPLE SEED

IS PLANTED IN THE GROUND

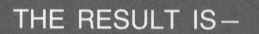

THE RESULT IS—

16   MANY, MANY APPLES.

LIKE THE APPLE THE THREE PERSONS OF THE

1 TRUE GOD HAVE DIFFERENT PURPOSES TOO.

GOD THE FATHER

IS OUR PROTECTOR.

HE MADE US—

YOU

ME

ALL PEOPLE

ALL THINGS

EVEN APPLES

HE LOVES US AND PROTECTS US, MAKES EVEN BAD THINGS TURN OUT FOR OUR GOOD.

HE KEEPS THINGS GROWING SO WE HAVE FOOD—

COWS

CARROTS

EVEN APPLES

19

SOMETIMES WE DO THINGS
THAT GOD DOESN'T LIKE.

GOD SAID THERE MUST BE A

PUNISHMENT FOR THESE THINGS.

THAT WOULD
MAKE US
VERY SAD.

IT WOULD
HURT A LOT

FOR A VERY
LONG, LONG
TIME.

BUT GOD LOVES US SO MUCH
HE SENT

GOD THE SON

TO TAKE OUR PUNISHMENT FOR US.

HIS NAME IS
JESUS.

HE WAS A REAL
MAN.

HE SUFFERED.

IT HURT A LOT.

HE DIED.

JESUS WAS BURIED

AS AN APPLE SEED IS BURIED

IN THE GROUND.

24

BUT HE WAS REALLY GOD
AND AS AN APPLE SEED SPROUTS FROM THE
GROUND AND MAKES NEW APPLES POSSIBLE,

JESUS ROSE

FROM THE DEAD

AND THE RESULT IS

BEAUTIFUL, WONDERFUL, HAPPY NEW LIVES FOR US.

BUT BEFORE WE CAN HAVE THIS

BEAUTIFUL

WONDERFUL

HAPPINESS

THERE IS
SOMETHING ELSE
WE MUST HAVE —

FAITH IN JESUS.

WHEN YOU PLANT AN APPLE SEED IN THE GROUND,
YOU BELIEVE
AN APPLE TREE WILL GROW FROM IT.

THAT'S FAITH
IN AN APPLE SEED.

WHEN YOU BELIEVE
JESUS DIED FOR YOU AND LIVES AGAIN
TO GIVE YOU A BEAUTIFUL, WONDERFUL, HAPPY
NEW LIFE,

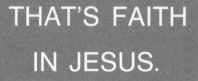

THAT'S FAITH

IN JESUS.

OUR HEARTS ARE LIKE A PIECE OF GROUND.

THE GROUND CANNOT PLANT ITSELF
WITH AN APPLE SEED.

SOMEONE MUST PUT THE SEED
INTO THE GROUND.

WE CANNOT PUT FAITH INTO OUR OWN HEARTS.

GOD THE HOLY SPIRIT

MAKES US BELIEVE IN JESUS.

HE PUTS FAITH
INTO OUR HEARTS

AND KEEPS IT
ALIVE AND GROWING

AS LONG AS WE
WANT HIM TO.

WHEN
AN
APPLE
SEED
IS
PLANTED
IN
THE
GROUND,
THE
RAIN
FEEDS
IT,
AND
IT
BEGINS
TO
GROW.

WHEN THE HOLY SPIRIT PUTS FAITH INTO THE HEART,
HE FEEDS IT WITH GOD'S WORD, AND

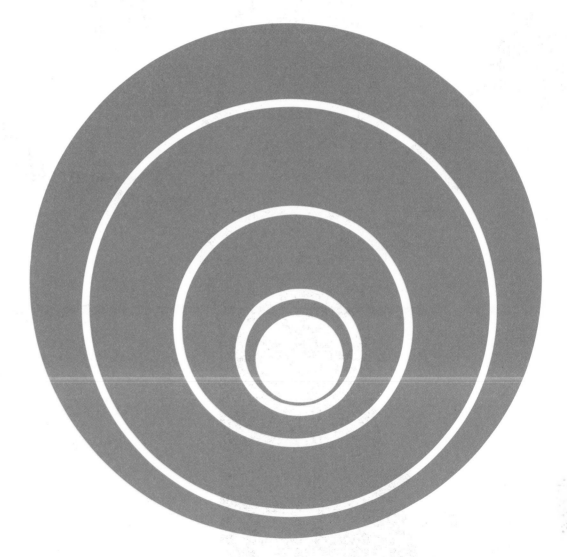

FAITH BEGINS TO GROW.

WHEN THE APPLE
TREE IS GROWN UP
STRONG AND HEALTHY,
IT BEARS FRUIT:

APPLES

WHEN FAITH IS
GROWN UP STRONG
AND HEALTHY, IT
BEARS FRUIT TOO:

JOY

HUMILITY

PATIENCE

GOODNESS

LOVE

KINDNESS

SELF-CONTROL

PEACE

FAITHFULNESS

WHEN YOU PICK AN APPLE FROM A TREE,
YOU KNOW IT IS AN APPLE.

IT LOOKS LIKE AN APPLE.

IT HAS AN APPLE PEEL.

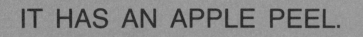

ITS FLESH IS APPLE.

IF YOU PLANT A SEED
FROM ITS CORE,
AN APPLE TREE WILL GROW.

THOUGH IT HAS THREE PARTS,
YOU KNOW YOU DO NOT HAVE THREE APPLES.

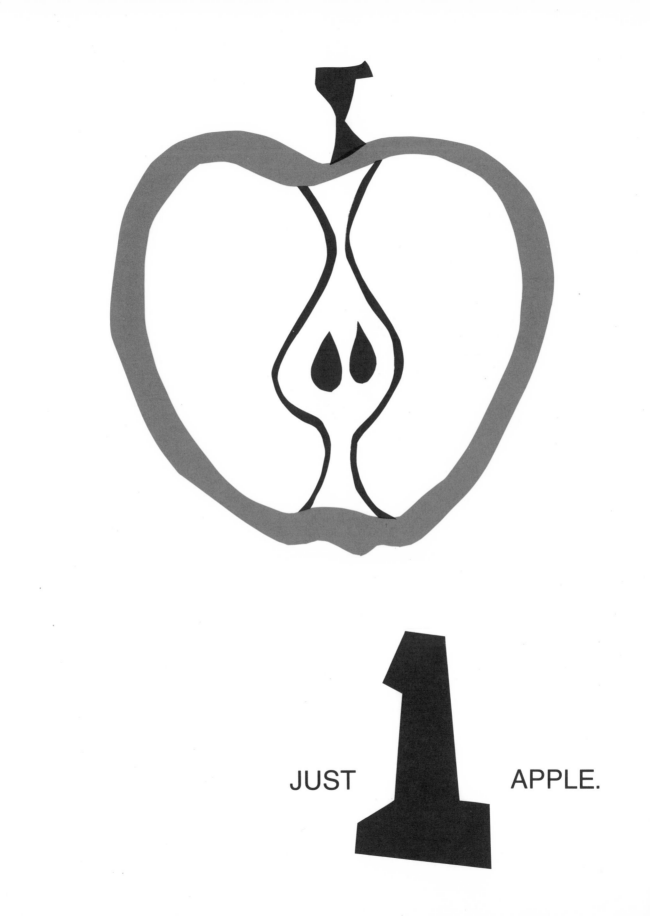

JUST 1 APPLE.

IF YOU HAVE FAITH IN THE TRUE GOD,
YOU BELIEVE IN

GOD THE FATHER

GOD THE SON

GOD
THE HOLY SPIRIT.

THERE ARE THREE PERSONS.

BUT THERE IS ONLY 1 TRUE GOD.